Wild Life™ LOL!

Great White Sharks

Hi! Nice to SEA you.

SCHOLASTIC

Library of Congress Cataloging-in-Publication Data
Title: Great white sharks
Description: New York: Children's Press, an imprint of Scholastic Inc., 2020. | Series: Wild life LOL! | Includes index.
Identifiers: LCCN 2019009539| ISBN 9780531240373 (library binding) | ISBN 9780531234907 (pbk.)
Subjects: LCSH: White shark—Juvenile literature. | Sharks—Juvenile literature.
Classification: LCC QL638.95.L3 G727 2020 | DDC 597.3/3—dc23

Produced by Spooky Cheetah Press

Design by Anna Tunick Tabachnik

Contributing Editor and Jokester: Pamela Chanko

Printed in Heshan, China 62

SCHOLASTIC, CHILDREN'S PRESS, WILD LIFE LOL!™, and associated logos are trademarks and/or registered trademarks of
Scholastic Inc.

1 2 3 4 5 6 7 8 9 10 R 29 28 27 26 25 24 23 22 21 20

Scholastic Inc., 557 Broadway, New York, NY 10012.

Photographs ©: cover, spine: Brandon Cole Marine Photography; cover speech bubbles and throughout: pijama61/iStockphoto; cover
speech bubbles and throughout: Astarina/Shutterstock; back cover and throughout: Rodrigo Friscione/Getty Images; 1 and throughout:
Dave Fleetham/Getty Images; 3 bottom and throughout: Reinhard Dirscherl/ullstein bild/Getty Images; 4: Chris and Monique Fallows/
Minden Pictures; 5 child silo: Nowik Sylwia/Shutterstock; 10-11: Ken Kiefer 2/Getty Images; 11 bottom right: Benjamin Lowy/Getty
Images; 12: Chris and Monique Fallows/Minden Pictures; 13 top left: AlinaMD/iStockphoto; 13 top right: Mark Fitzpatrick/EyeEm/Getty
Images; 13 bottom left: Gerard Soury/Exactostock/Superstock, Inc.; 13 bottom right: Federico Cabello/SuperStock, Inc.; 14: Jennifer
Hayes/Getty Images; 15: Sergey Uryadnikov/Shutterstock; 16: Denis Scott/Getty Images; 17 left: Chris and Monique Fallows/Minden
Pictures; 17 right: C & M Fallows/SeaPics.com; 18-19: Pascal Kobeh/NPL/Minden Pictures; 20-21: Cultura Exclusive/Rodrigo Friscione/
Getty Images; 22-23: Robert Snow/OCEARCH; 24-25: Jeff Gage/Florida Museum of Natural History; 26 left: Musée du Quai Branly/
Jacques Chirac Dist. RMN-Grand Palais/Art Resource, NY; 26 right: Scott Dickerson/Getty Images; 27 right: Chris and Monique Fallows/
Minden Pictures; 28 top: Bruce Rasner/Jeffrey Rotman/Biosphoto; 28 bottom: Alex Mustard/Nature Picture Library/Alamy Images;
29 top: wildestanimal/Shutterstock; 29 center: Doug Perrine/NPL/Minden Pictures; 29 bottom: Daniela Dirscherl/Getty Images;
30 map: Jim McMahon/Mapman®; 31 top: Denis Scott/Getty Images; 32: Ken Kiefer 2/Getty Images; 34: Jennifer Hayes/Getty Images;
35: Sergey Uryadnikov/Shutterstock.

TABLE OF CONTENTS

Wow! This is killer!

MEET THE
FEARSOME GREAT WHITE SHARK

Are you ready to be amazed and amused? Keep reading! This book is FIN-tastic!

LOL!
Why don't sharks like to eat clown fish? **Because they taste funny.**

Blastoff!

At a Glance

Where do they live? → Great white sharks live in open ocean and coastal areas around the world.

What do they do? → Great white sharks cruise the oceans in search of their next meal.

What do they eat? → Great whites eat seals and sea lions, as well as fish, seabirds, squid, and turtles.

What do they look like? → Great white sharks have torpedo-shaped bodies with huge jaws and sharp teeth.

How big are they? →

HINT: You're smaller. Check this out:

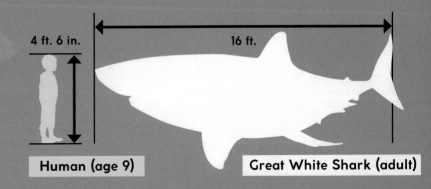

4 ft. 6 in.

16 ft.

Human (age 9)

Great White Shark (adult)

AT HOME IN THE DEEP

Great white sharks are fish, so they live in water. They are found all over the world.

One Fast Fish

Great white sharks are fast swimmers! That's partly because the shark's body is super flexible. It has no bones. A shark's skeleton is made of **cartilage**—just like your outer ears!

THAT'S EXTREME!
Great white sharks can swim thousands of miles in a year.

So Cool, They're Hot

Sharks don't mind swimming in chilly water. Unlike other fish, great whites can raise their body temperature.

Underwater Breathers
Water flows through a shark's gills as it swims. These slits in the shark's sides pull oxygen from the water.

cartilage: a strong, elastic body tissue

A GREAT WHITE'S BODY

This top **predator** is built to rule Earth's oceans!

WACKY FACT:
Each shark has unique markings on its larger top fin—like a FIN-gerprint!

THAT'S EXTREME!
A great white can go through up to 50,000 teeth in a lifetime!

That's the Tooth!
Sharks have many rows of teeth. If they lose a tooth in front, a tooth from behind moves up to take its place.

predator: an animal that hunts other animals for food

Balancing Act

The shark has two fins on the top of its body. They help it balance. Two fins on the sides help the shark steer.

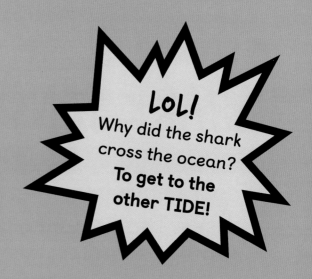

LOL!
Why did the shark cross the ocean? **To get to the other TIDE!**

Tale of the Tail

A shark's tail fin provides explosive speed. It helps this ocean hunter swim as fast as 35 miles per hour.

Blending In

The shark's white underside blends in with the bright sky. It helps keep the shark hidden from **prey** below.

prey: an animal that is killed by another animal for food

SHARK SENSE

Sharks have very sharp senses. That is part of what makes them such great hunters!

THAT'S EXTREME!
A great white can smell a colony of seals 2 miles away.

The Eyes (and Ears) Have It
Sharks have very good vision, even where there's little light—like in deep water! They also have excellent hearing.

snout: the animal body part that includes the nose, mouth, and jaws

Super Sniffer
Great whites have an excellent sense of smell. They can sniff out one drop of blood in 10 billion drops of water!

LOL!
What do you get when you cross a great white with a snowman?
Frostbite!

Hmm . . . I think I smell something fishy!

Secret of the Snout
Pores on the shark's **snout** can pick up electric impulses sent out by prey.

WHAT'S FOR DINNER?

Great whites are meat-eaters. They like seals and sea lions best. But sharks eat other foods, too, including parts of dead whales!

THAT'S EXTREME!
On average, great white sharks can eat 11 tons of food in a single year. That's like eating more than 80,000 fishburgers!

WACKY FACT:
A great white that has just eaten can wait two months until its next meal.

Pleased to EAT you!

sea birds

sea turtles

These animals are also part of a shark's diet.

fish

squid

ON THE HUNT

Great whites have two main ways to hunt.

WACKY FACT: A great white has a bite force four times as strong as a lion's.

1
the sneak attack

Is there someone behind me?

Shhh . . .
The great white swims up from underneath the animal or sneaks in from behind.

Gotcha!
With two flicks of its tail fin, the shark shoots forward and grabs its meal.

THAT'S EXTREME!
A great white can jump 10 feet out of the water. That's as high as a basketball hoop!

Swish!

2
the jump shot

Eye Spy...

The shark pokes its head above the water to look for prey.

Dinner!

The shark races up through the water, leaps out into the air, and grabs the prey in its teeth.

A KILLER SMILE

The great white has a killer bite. Here's how it works.

LOL!
What's a shark's least favorite candy?
Jawbreakers!

1

Open Wide

A great white's jaw isn't attached to its skull, so it can open its mouth really wide. To grab large prey, the shark lifts its snout high and drops its lower jaw.

Here's something I can sink my teeth into!

WACKY FACT: When a great white shark attacks, its eyes roll back in its head for protection.

② Say Aaah . . .

The shark pushes its entire jaw forward, revealing rows of triangular teeth. Each tooth has edges that cut like a knife. They are made for biting, not chewing.

③ Crunch!

The shark grabs its prey with its teeth. The shark swallows small prey whole. If the prey is big, the shark bites off large chunks and swallows those.

LET'S GET TOGETHER

Scientists don't know a lot about how great whites start families. Here's what they think happens.

LOL!
Why do sharks swim in salt water?
Because pepper water makes them sneeze!

1

Ocean Clubhouse

A spot in the Pacific Ocean seems to be a favorite meeting place for great whites.

WACKY FACT:
A male shark is ready to mate when it is about 10 years old.

I need a mate. I'd better CHEWS wisely!

2

Come On Over

In late spring and summer, groups of males come to the spot to search for females.

3

The Gang's All Here

Females float into the area, staying just long enough to join with a male.

SECRETS OF THE SEA

No one on Earth has ever seen a great white shark give birth! Scientists do know a few things about how the babies are born, though.

EGGS-traordinary
Most fish lay eggs, but not great white sharks. Their eggs hatch inside their bodies! Their babies, called pups, are born alive.

Where do you think we come from?

Cheaper by the Dozen

Most female great whites have two to 10 eggs in a litter. Each egg develops within a special pouch inside the female.

Hmm . . . is it FIN-land?

First Come, First Served

On average, fewer than half of the pups in the litter are born. Scientists think the first to hatch may eat the other eggs inside their mother.

PUP, PUP, HURRAY!

In 2016, researchers were able to track nine great white pups.

Found You!
Researchers spotted the baby sharks in the shallow waters off the coast of Long Island. They think the pups were born in that part of the Atlantic Ocean.

Big Babies
Newborn great whites are about 4 feet long and weigh 30 to 50 pounds. That's about the size of a first grader.

On Their Own
The pups swim away from their mother as soon as they are born. Luckily, the pups already know how to hunt!

ANCIENT SHARKS

The Hubbell's white shark is the oldest ancestor of the great white. Scientists know this because they have found **fossils** like this one.

THAT'S EXTREME!
Sharks lived on Earth way before the dinosaurs—and they're still here!

One of a Kind
This fossil is a complete set of jaws with 222 teeth. It's the only intact partial skull of this shark that's ever been found.

GREAT WHITE
Carcharodon ca
This 5 million year
was collected in Sac
February, 1988. The t
the specimen is esti
about 6 meters. Th
complete fossilized sk
White shark that ha
recovered.

fossils: plants or animals from millions of years ago preserved as rock

GREAT WHITES AND PEOPLE

We have a long—and complicated—history!

This is a statue of a shark god.

Long Ago

Some ancient cultures told stories of sharks that protected fishermen. They were shark gods. Humans didn't hunt sharks in large numbers—yet.

1970s and '80s

People cut off sharks' fins to make soup. Some sharks were caught for sport. Others accidentally drowned when they were caught in fishing nets.

2013

A report was published that said that about 100 million sharks were being killed every year. Countries started working to protect them.

Today

It's not possible to say exactly how many great white sharks live in the wild. But experts believe their numbers continue to increase.

Great White Cousins

These are some of the great white's closest relatives.

Wait . . . are you saying I have a big mouth?

megamouth shark

I'm the second-largest fish in the world.

basking shark

Please note: Animals are not shown to scale.

The Wild Life

Look at this map of the world. The areas with red stripes show where great white sharks live today. We want our great white sharks to continue having clean waters to live in. We need to protect their **habitats**.

Pacific Ocean

Atlantic Ocean

Pacific Ocean

Let's keep it clean!

habitats: the places where a plant or an animal makes its home

An Island of Plastic

Have you heard about the Great Pacific Garbage Patch? It is a huge area of the Pacific Ocean—between California and Hawaii—where marine litter collects. It contains almost 80,000 tons of plastic.

Plastic bags, bottles, and straws and small bits of plastic float in the patch. Abandoned fishing nets and other gear can entangle and kill ocean animals. All this litter threatens wildlife, including great white sharks.

What Can You Do?

Try to create less waste, especially plastic. Do your part by saying "no thank you" to a plastic straw next time you eat out. Or talk to your parents about buying a reusable straw that you can take with you to restaurants. Learn about and remember to always practice the three Rs: reduce, reuse, and recycle.

ABOUT THIS BOOK

This is a laugh-out-loud early-grade adaptation of
Great White Sharks by Moira Rose Donohue, originally published
by Scholastic as part of its Nature's Children series in 2018.

SEA you soon!